bala
kids

An imprint of **Shambhala Publications, Inc.**
2129 13th Street
Boulder, Colorado 80302
www.shambhala.com

9 8 7 6 5 4 3 2 1

First Edition
Printed in China

This edition is printed on acid-free paper that meets the American National Standards Institute Z39.48 Standard.

Shambhala Publications makes every effort to print on recycled paper.
For more information please visit www.shambhala.com.
Bala Kids is distributed worldwide by **Penguin Random House, Inc.**, and its subsidiaries.

Library of Congress Cataloging-in-Publication Data
Names: Gruhl, Jason, author. | Font, Ignasi, illustrator.
Title: Just a thought / Jason Gruhl; illustrations by Ignasi Font.
Description: First edition. | Boulder, Colorado: Shambhala, 2021. |
Audience: Ages 4–8 | Audience: Grades K–1
Identifiers: LCCN 2020021238 | ISBN 9781611808605 (hardback)
Subjects: LCSH: Thought and thinking—Juvenile literature.
Classification: LCC B105.T54 G78 2021 | DDC 153.4/2—dc23
LC record available at https://lccn.loc.gov/2020021238

JUST a THOUGHT

JASON GRUHL

ILLUSTRATED BY

IGNASI FONT

EXPLORING YOUR WEIRD, WACKY, AND WONDERFUL MIND!

IT CRASHED INTO ANOTHER THOUGHT—
THE SCARED AND WORRIED KIND!

THEN AN ANGRY THOUGHT BLAZED IN.
IT WASN'T VERY NICE.

BUT IT GOT SQUASHED BY *TWO* SAD THOUGHTS
THAT MADE THAT THOUGHT THINK TWICE.

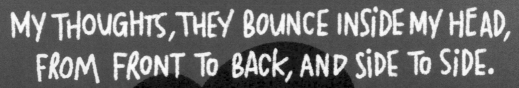

MY THOUGHTS, THEY BOUNCE INSIDE MY HEAD,
FROM FRONT TO BACK, AND SIDE TO SIDE.

MY MIND, IT MAKES THEM DAY AND NIGHT.
DO I CREATE THEM ALL?

SOME THOUGHTS ARE HELPFUL
OR MAKE US DARING.

SOME THOUGHTS PROTECT
AND KEEP US CARING.

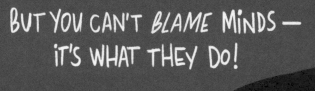

BUT YOU CAN'T *BLAME* MINDS —
IT'S WHAT THEY DO!

THEY THINK UP THOUGHTS
TO BURP AND SPEW.

THEY TAKE SHORT BREAKS,
BUT THOSE DON'T LAST....

THEY *LOVE* TO THINK
A THINK-THOUGHT BLAST!

So WHY, SOMETIMES, CAN I *SEE* MY THOUGHTS AND WATCH THEM LIKE A STORY?

WHILE OTHER DAYS I'M *LOST* IN THOUGHT, IN MIXED-UP TERRITORY?

I WONDER IF I'M *NOT* MY THOUGHTS,
IF *I* AM SOMETHING MORE...

SOMETHING
IN A BODY
WITH A MIND I CAN

EXPLORE?

PERHAPS I'M LiKE THE BiG BLUE SKY,
NO END iN SiGHT, A MiLE HiGH.

AND THOUGHTS ARE PUFFY, FLUFFY CLOUDS
THAT FLOAT AND DRiFT ON BY.

OR MAYBE I'M THE MASSIVE OCEAN,
DEEP AND WIDE, A CONSTANT NOTION.

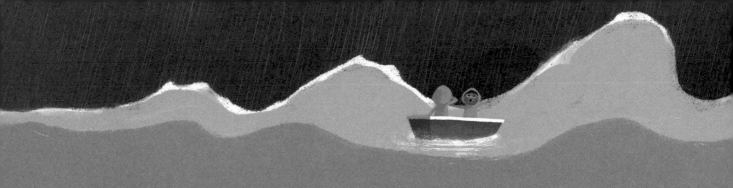

AND THOUGHTS ARE LiKE THE WAVES UP TOP,
A STORMY, LOUD COMMOTION.

OR ARE MY THOUGHTS
LIKE FUZZY SHEEP

THAT PRANCE AND WANDER,
BOUND AND LEAP?

AND I AM AN ENORMOUS MOUNTAIN—
STEADY, STRONG, AND STEEP.

OR MAYBE I AM CLEAR, VAST SPACE.
I'M EVERYTHING AND EVERY PLACE!

AND THOUGHTS ARE WHIZZING, SHOOTING STARS
THAT FLEE WITHOUT A TRACE.

OUR THOUGHTs, iT SEEMS,
ARE *LiTTLE* THINGS
WHiLE WE ARE GRAND
AND SPACiOUS.

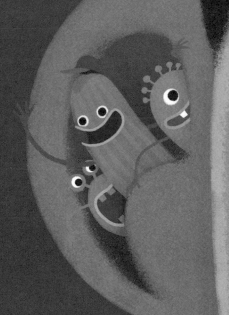

THE MIND CAN DANCE IN EMPTINESS
AND PAINT WITH LIGHT AND FIRE...

CAN WRITE NEW TALES
AND SING NEW SONGS.

WHAT *ELSE* CAN MIND INSPIRE?

MOST THOUGHTS CAN JUST BE LEFT ALONE—
NO NEED TO JUDGE OR FEAR.

HOW PEACEFUL WOULD OUR MINDS BE THEN?
HOW RESTFUL, CALM, AND CLEAR!

IN QUIET, WE CAN FINALLY HEAR WHAT THERE *REALLY* IS TO DO.
AND LIFE CAN HELP AND SPEAK ITS TRUTH,
IT MOVES AND ACTS THROUGH YOU.

I GUESS iT'S GONE.
iT PASSED ON THROUGH.

OH WELL... iT'S JUST A THOUGHT.

AUTHOR'S NOTE

THOUGHTS ARE RUNNING THROUGH OUR HEADS ALL DAY LONG, AND IT'S EASY TO FEEL LIKE WE *HAVE* TO LISTEN TO THEM, ESPECIALLY WHEN THERE ARE A LOT OF THEM OR WHEN THEY'RE LOUD.

BUT THE TRUTH IS, YOU'RE *BIGGER* THAN THOUGHTS—YOU ARE THE ONE *WATCHING* THEM. AND BECAUSE OF THAT, YOU GET TO DECIDE WHAT TO DO WITH THEM. SOMETIMES YOU *NEED* TO LISTEN TO THEM, LIKE IF ONE TELLS YOU *NOT* TO KISS A CROCODILE. PLEASE LISTEN TO THAT THOUGHT! BUT MOST OF THE TIME IT'S OKAY TO SAY, "THANKS ANYWAY, THOUGHT. I'VE GOT THIS." IT CAN BE HARD TO TELL THE DIFFERENCE SOMETIMES, BUT WITH A LITTLE PRACTICE, YOU'LL FIGURE IT OUT, AND IN THE PROCESS, YOU'LL GET TO KNOW YOUR BEAUTIFUL MIND...

AND THAT'S A WONDERFUL THOUGHT.

MEDITATION: SKY, OCEAN, MOUNTAIN, SPACE
(3-5 + MINUTES)

MEDITATION HELPS YOU GET TO KNOW YOUR MIND: HOW IT WORKS AND WHAT THOUGHTS LIKE TO PASS THROUGH IT. IN THIS MEDITATION, YOU'LL GET TO RELAX, BREATHE DEEPLY, AND WATCH YOUR THOUGHTS FROM THE VIEW OF THE SKY, AN OCEAN, A MOUNTAIN, OR OUTER SPACE— WHICHEVER YOU CHOOSE!

1 SIT ON A CUSHION OR LIE DOWN ON THE FLOOR. NOW CLOSE YOUR EYES AND RELAX YOUR BODY.

2 TAKE A DEEP BREATH IN AND FILL YOUR BELLY WITH AIR LIKE YOU'RE BLOWING UP A BALLOON. THEN SLOWLY BREATHE OUT THROUGH YOUR NOSE.

3 CONTINUE TO BREATHE AND RELAX. PRETEND THAT YOU ARE THE SKY, AN OCEAN, A MOUNTAIN, OR OUTER SPACE.

4 WATCH AS YOUR THOUGHTS PASS THROUGH YOUR MIND LIKE CLOUDS, WAVES, SHEEP, OR STARS. JUST NOTICE YOUR THOUGHTS WITHOUT TRYING TO CHANGE THEM:
→ YOU MIGHT HEAR SOUNDS.
→ YOU MIGHT SMELL FOOD.
→ YOU MIGHT START THINKING ABOUT WHAT YOU'LL DO AFTER SCHOOL.
→ YOU MIGHT THINK ABOUT YOUR DOG OR CAT.
BUT, AGAIN, JUST NOTICE THE THOUGHTS AND LET THEM PASS ON BY.

5 CONTINUE TO BREATHE DEEPLY AND RELAX, FILLING YOUR BELLY ... AND THEN LETTING THE AIR OUT SLOWLY THROUGH YOUR NOSE.

OPEN YOUR EYES. SHARE SOME OF THE THOUGHTS YOU NOTICED WITH A TEACHER, FAMILY MEMBER, FRIEND, OR CLASSMATE. DID ANYTHING SURPRISE YOU? IF YOU ARE NOT YOUR THOUGHTS, WHAT ARE YOU? DO YOU THINK EVERYONE HAS THOUGHTS LIKE YOURS?

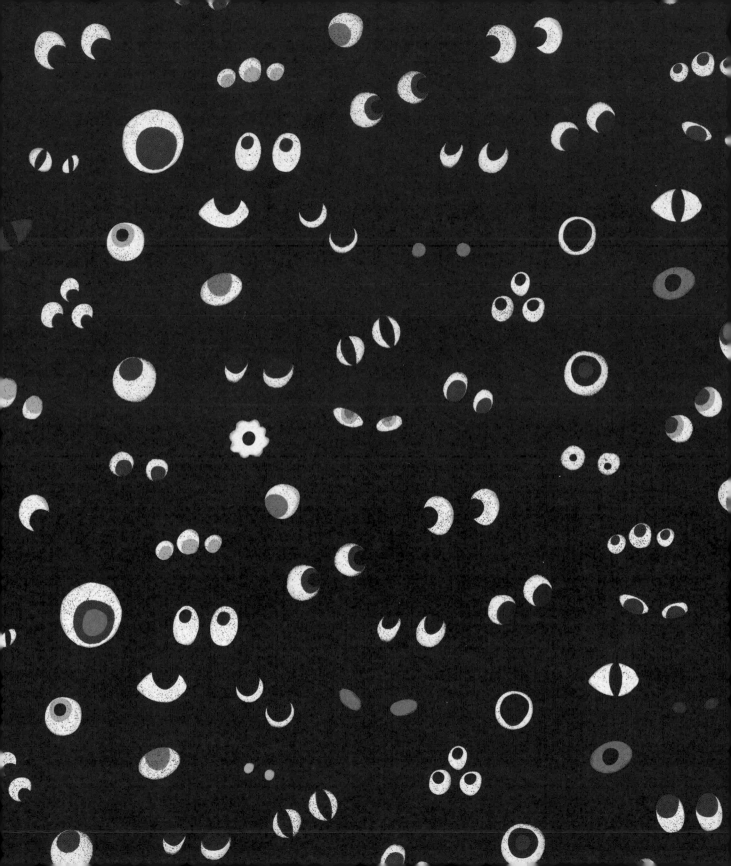